Go Strollers !!

Family trip to National Park 01
Mount Rainier National Park

Go Strollers !!
- Family Trip to National Park 01 -

Mount Rainier National Park

About Us

We are a couple with two boys (ages 7 and 5) living in Seattle. We came to Seattle in 2008 to study at the University of Washington and since then have fallen in love with the natural beauty of the area and enjoy exploring the many beautiful sites around Washington state and national parks in the US.

From Yellowstone National Park, the first national park established in 1872 to Pinnacles National Park, the most recent one designated as a national park in 2013, there are 59 national parks in the United States. We would like to share our experience at each park for families like us planning to visit national parks with young kids.

Mount Rainier National Park is the first national park that we have visited. Previously we only made day trips to the park 2 to 3 times each year, but in the summer of 2016 we stayed near the park for 5 days and explored many of the park's attractions.

In this book, we have organized a summary of our family's trip including a brief journal of our journey, information that we researched before the trip, tips that we realized would be good to know and pictures. Because this trip is focused on travelling with young children, the difficulty level is mostly based on 'easy' courses with a couple of 'moderately challenging' attractions.

Therefore, regardless of the size of your family or the ages of your children, it is simple to think of the attractions in this book as a trip that a five-year-old enjoyed. If you find any incorrect information, typos, or any content that otherwise needs to be revised, please feel free to contact us at info@gostrollers.com.

Feb 10 2017
KJ & Maria

Trip to Mount Rainier National Park

Explore the iconic landmark of the State of Washington. Enjoy the subalpine meadows with abundance of wildflowers, magnificent glaciers, crystal clear rivers, stunning waterfalls, ancient old-growth forests, and the beautiful hiking trails across the park.

Getting There
Nisqually Entrance, Mount Rainier National Park
39000 State Route 706 E, Ashford, WA 98304
※ This entrance is the closest to the two most visited attractions, Paradise and Longmire

Distance and Travel Time (from downtown Seattle) 86 miles (2h)

Admission
$25 per car for up to 15 people for 7 days. If you purchase the interagency annual pass for $80, you can get unlimited access to all National Parks and Federal Recreational sites within the US.

When to Go
Jun to Oct (The park is partially open in winter also, but may be a difficult trip with young kids. August is usually the best season to see abundance of wildflowers but its peak bloom varies each year.)

Our Itinerary

Letter A) to L) are indicated on the right map.

Day 1: Tipsoo Lake
A) Naches Peak Loop Trail, Tipsoo Lake

K) Hotel in *Buckley

* You can find retailers, grocery stores & a Starbucks in Buckley.

Day 2: Sunrise
B) Sunrise Nature Trail & Silver Forest Trail, Sunrise

K) Hotel in Buckley

Day 3: Ohanapecosh & Stevens Canyon Road
C) Silver Falls Loop Trail & Grove of the Patriarchs, Ohanapecosh

D) Box Canyon Loop Trail, Stevens Canyon Road

L) Hotel in Packwood

Day 4: Paradise & Longmire
E) Skyline Trail up to Glacier Vista, Paradise

F) Trail of the Shadows, Longmire

L) Hotel in Packwood

Day 5: Stevens Canyon Road, Longmire & Carbon/Mowich
G) Reflection Lakes & Louise Lake, Stevens Canyon Road

H) Narada Falls, Longmire

I) Mowich Lake

J) Rainforest Nature Trail, Carbon River

Our Itinerary

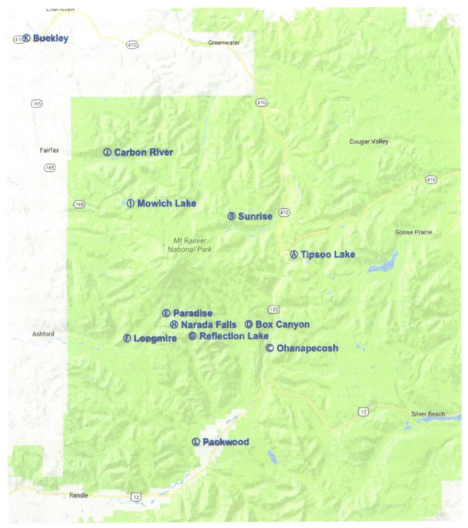

Tips

1) Even when it's sunny in Seattle, the Mt. Rainier area can be much different so be sure to check the park website and <u>webcams</u> for current conditions and also check the **weather forecast** for the Mt. Rainier area before departing.

2) The weather in the mountains changes frequently so **dress in layers** to be prepared.

3) If your family is not used to spending long hours in the car, make it an **overnight trip** and spend a night near the park.

4) **Kid-safe bug repellent** can be useful to keep bugs away.

1) Tipsoo Lake Area

The Adventure

Explore the Naches Peak Loop Trail which starts at Tipsoo Lake and is one of the most popular easy trails at Mount Rainier with magnificent views of the mountain, beautiful small lakes and abundance of wildflowers in summer.

Getting There

Naches Peak Loop Trailhead, Tipsoo Lake, Mount Rainier

28143 Washington 410, Naches, WA 98937

Tips

1) The **Naches Peak Loop Trail** is **3.5 miles (5.5 km)** long with an **elevation gain of 500 feet**.

2) Start your hike on the Naches Peak Loop Trail **clockwise** for best views of Mount Rainier.

3) The **Tipsoo Lake trail** is an easy **0.5 mile** trail around the lake.

Naches Peak Loop Trail Map

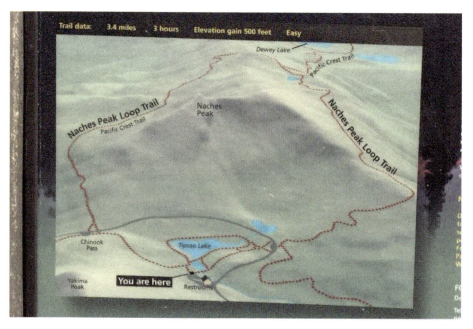

1) Naches Peak Loop Trail, Tipsoo Lake

We started our adventure at Tipsoo Lake on the east side of Mount Rainier.

The Naches Peak Loop trail is a popular easy to moderate trail famous for picturesque views of Mount Rainier and beautiful wildflowers. The roads in this area are closed in winter, thus only accessible in summer.

1) Naches Peak Loop Trail, Tipsoo Lake

Although the trail may be a little long at 3.5 miles (5.6km), the elevation gain is only 500ft (150m) making it a nice trip for families with kids.

While it takes the average person about 2 hours to walk the complete loop, we took our time and completed the trail in 4 hours, talking with the children and encouraging each other along the way.

1) Naches Peak Loop Trail, Tipsoo Lake

The small lake along the trail was a nice stop for a rest. Some people even enjoyed swimming there.

Strolling along the beautiful trail surrounded by wildflowers was truly a refreshing experience for all of us.

1) Naches Peak Loop Trail, Tipsoo Lake

Hundreds of species of wildflowers bloom in the subalpine meadows of Mount Rainier National Park. Lupines are among those that paint the meadows during summer.

Lupines are known as a favorite of the blacktailed deer that roam the area.

1) Naches Peak Loop Trail, Tipsoo Lake

After about half-way along the loop, a breathtaking view of Mount Rainier can be seen right in front of you.

This picturesque view was well-worth the hours of walking.

2) Sunrise Area

The Adventure

Explore the highest point reachable by car at Mount Rainier National Park and enjoy breathtaking views of Emmons glacier - the largest surface area of any glacier in the contiguous United States.

Getting There

Sunrise Visitor Center, Mount Rainier

Sunrise Park Rd, Ashford, WA 98304

Tips

There are 2 easy trails that the whole family can enjoy with majestic views. They are indicated on the right map in red/blue.

Sunrise Nature Trail (1.5 miles, 300ft elevation gain)

- Most of the trail is wide allowing for side-by-side hiking
- Start at the north trailhead and make a right at the fork and continue up until you meet the fork for the **Sourdough Ridge Trail** and **Dege Peak**. Turn left towards the Sourdough Ridge Trail which is the northern part of the loop. Continue until you meet the next fork in the trail. Make another left to head back towards Sunrise.
- The first part of the trail has **mileposts** which can be good motivation for little ones to walk on to find the next one.

Silver Forest Trail (2 miles, 150ft elevation gain)

- Most of the trail is narrower (more towards the end).
- **Emmons Vista Overlook** which can be reached by the first 0.5 miles along the **Silver Forest Trail** can be a good turning point for those not wanting to walk the whole trail.

2) Sunrise Area

Junior Ranger Program

Kids preschool age and up may enjoy participating in the **Junior Ranger program** to earn a **Junior Ranger badge**. Ask for a junior ranger activity book at the visitor center.

Sunrise Area Trail Map

Source: http://www.nps.gov/mora/planyourvisit/upload/sunrise-area-trails-aug11-2.pdf

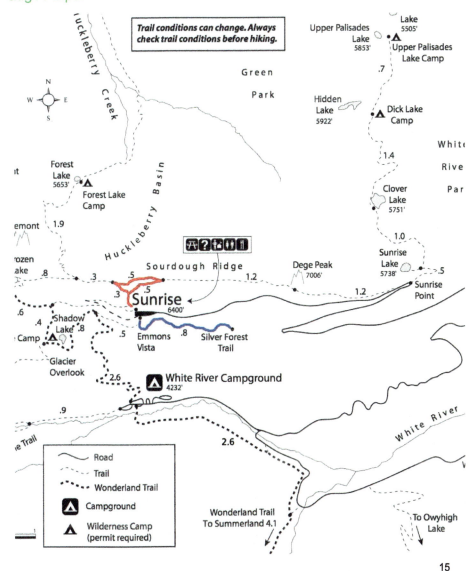

2-1) Sunrise Point

On day 2, we went to Sunrise, the highest point at Mount Rainier National Park that is accessible by car.

At Sunrise Point, which has a parking area slightly before reaching Sunrise, you can enjoy views of both Mount Rainier and Mt. Adams in the distance on clear days.

2-2) *Sunrise Point to Sunrise*

The elevation of this area is 6,400ft (1,950m) and the views of the mountain feels closer, offering a majestic experience.

Another 1.2 miles past Sunrise Point leads to Sunrise where you can find trailheads to many different trails and enjoy the views.

2-3) Sunrise Nature Trail, Sunrise

A big meadow covers the northern side of Sunrise. Walk up the trail along the left side of the meadow to reach the trailhead to the Sunrise Nature Trail and many other trails that extend from it.

The Sunrise Nature Trail is not explicitly shown on the trail map, but it is the small loop that starts from the trailhead. Follow the right uphill trail from the trailhead to walk this trail.

2-3) *Sunrise Nature Trail, Sunrise*

There are mileposts along the first part of this trail which is fun for the kids to look for.

0.5 miles along the trail, you reach a fork. The right side heads towards Dege Peak, while the left heads towards Sourdough Ridge trail. Take the left trail to walk the loop back to the trailhead.

2-3) Sunrise Nature Trail, Sunrise

At this fork you can enjoy the view of Mount Baker and the mountains along the Cascade Range in the distance.

From this point, which is about 300ft (90m) higher than the Sunrise parking area, you can enjoy the views of the majestic Emmons Glacier and the vast subalpine meadows.

2-3) *Sunrise Nature Trail, Sunrise*

We took a moment to rest a bit while admiring the grandeur of Mount Rainier and the peace and serenity nature provides.

The wildflowers along the trail remind us of the power of nature and how life makes its way through even in harsh environments.

2-3) Sunrise Nature Trail, Sunrise

About a half mile along the Sourdough Ridge trail, you will reach another fork. Take a left to walk back to the first trailhead.

After completing our stroll, we went to the Sunrise Visitor Center to check out some exhibits and enjoyed a break while the children worked on their Junior Ranger program booklet.

2-4) Silver Forest Trail, Sunrise

Another trailhead begins on the southern part of the parking lot. The Silver Forest Trail is another easy trail that the whole family can enjoy.

Follow the trail from the southern trailhead for a half mile to reach the Emmons Vista Overlook.

2-4) Silver Forest Trail, Sunrise

From this overlook you can get a great view of the Emmons glacier and the White River.

Beyond the Emmons Vista Overlook, the trail gets narrower and leads you through a meadow with wildflowers on a journey back in time.

2-4) *Silver Forest Trail, Sunrise*

Along the trail, you can see the remnants of an old burned area mixed in the vegetation. These 'silver' trees are the remains of a fire that have been bleached white by the weather.

Some of these trees stand among the lush vegetation while others can be found lying along the trail.

2-4) Silver Forest Trail, Sunrise

The turnback point of the Silver Forest Trail is marked by a sign indicating the 'End of Maintained Trail.' The round trip distance is 2 miles (3.2km).

You can enjoy majestic views of the Emmons glacier and the valley below on the walk back.

2-4) *Silver Forest Trail, Sunrise*

The elevation gain of this trail is slight and the walk back offers a great vista with wildflowers along the path, making this trail an easy trip even for young children.

Watching your family walk hand in hand in front of you is a priceless memory to be cherished from these adventures.

3) Ohanapecosh Area

The Adventure

Enjoy the well-maintained forest trail alongside the Ohanapecosh river to the waterfall, explore the giant old trees along the river and cross the suspension bridge.

Getting There

Ohanapecosh Visitor Center, Randle, WA 98377

Tips

There is no sign for the Ohanapecosh Visitor Center on the main road of highway 123, so **look for the sign for directions to the Ohanapecosh campground** soon after passing the Stevens Canyon Entrance (heading south on highway 123) and turn right as soon as you pass that sign.

Silver Falls Loop Trail (2.7 miles, 300ft elevation gain)

- Stroll along the 0.3 mile **Hot Springs Nature Trail** that starts from the **Ohanapecosh Visitor Center** to continue onto the Silver Falls trail.

Grove of the Patriachs (1.3 miles, 100ft elevation gain)

- **The Grove of the Patriarchs** is just a 0.9 mile walk from Silver Falls, but the extra distance (making the round trip 5+ miles) may make it a harder trip for younger kids. Hiking the Silver Falls Loop and taking a rest at the Visitor Center before heading toward the Grove of the Patriarchs trailhead by car can be a good option.
- **Parking for the Grove of the Patriarchs is limited** so go early in the morning or in the later hours of the afternoon.

3) Ohanapecosh Area

Junior Ranger Program

Kids preschool age and up may enjoy participating in the **Junior Ranger program** to earn a **Junior Ranger badge**. Ask for a junior ranger activity book at the visitor center.

Ohanapecosh Area Trail Map

Source: https://www.nps.gov/mora/planyourvisit/upload/Ohanapecosh-Area-Trails-Aug11.pdf

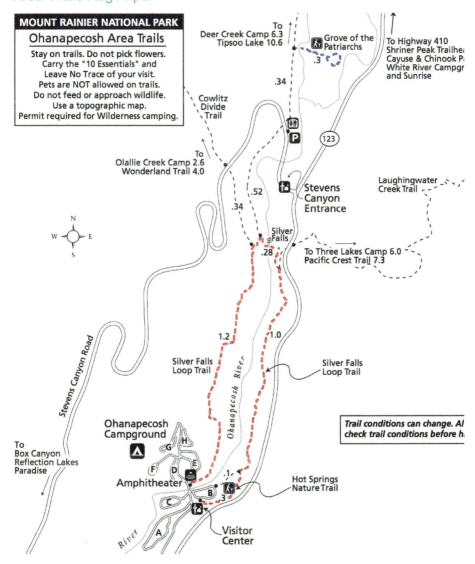

3-1) Silver Falls Loop Trail, Ohanapecosh

Mount Rainier is mostly known for the Paradise and Sunrise areas for magnificent views and wildflowers, but it also has a nice family-friendly forest area on the southeastern side that is less crowded.

We began our third day at the tranquil forest trail at Ohanapecosh. Ohanapecosh is thought to mean 'standing at the edge'.

3-1) Silver Falls Loop Trail, Ohanapecosh

Located at the southeastern part of the park, this area has a nice trail through an old-growth forest where you can see the Silver Falls and the clear waters of the Ohanapecosh river.

You can enjoy a refreshing stroll in the shade of the trees at a roundtrip of 2.7 miles (4.3km).

3-1) Silver Falls Loop Trail, Ohanapecosh

Ohanapecosh is less crowded than other more visited areas of the park making it feel like you are at a completely different place.

After about a mile (1.6km) past the 0.3 mile (0.48km) Hot Springs Nature Trail, you will reach the Laughingwater Creek where you cross a small bridge.

3-1) Silver Falls Loop Trail, Ohanapecosh

Soon after, you will hear the roar of the Silver Falls as you turn a corner to reach the viewpoint.

© GoStrollers.com

3-1) Silver Falls Loop Trail, Ohanapecosh

After crossing the bridge past the water from the falls, you will come to a fork leading either back towards the beginning of the loop or to a different trail for more hiking.

It is interesting to observe the contrast of the water from the footbridge.

3-1) Silver Falls Loop Trail, Ohanapecosh

On one side the water is strong and rough flowing down the falls, while on the other side it looks extremely calm and peaceful.

You can get a closer view of the falls at the Silver Falls Overlook which is on the right side of the trail past the bridge.

3-1) Silver Falls Loop Trail, Ohanapecosh

Continuing the walk along the loop, we took a short break to admire the huge rock wall on one side of the trail that looked as if it were from the primitive times.

We marvel at the wonders of nature and life as we see new trees growing from the remains of fallen trees.

3-1) Silver Falls Loop Trail, Ohanapecosh

The sun shines down on the children as they walk hand-in-hand, whispering fun thoughts to each other.

After completing the loop trail with ease (elevation gain is only 300ft (90m)), we checked out the exhibits in the visitor center to learn more about this area's ecosystem.

3-2) Grove of the Patriarchs, Ohanapecosh

The Grove of the Patriarchs is located right past the Stevens Canyon Entrance. You can also get there by walking another 0.9 mile (1.4km) from Silver Falls.

After a short walk along the trail you will get to a small suspension bridge over the Ohanapecosh river.

3-2) Grove of the Patriarchs, Ohanapecosh

The children enjoyed throwing rocks in the water at the riverside before moving on to the boardwalk trail.

The boardwalk is a loop trail surrounded by ancient giant trees. The kids merrily skipped along the loop many times.

3-2) Grove of the Patriarchs, Ohanapecosh

These ancient trees which have been standing for over a thousand years truly do live up to the namesake, the Patriarchs.

© GoStrollers.com

3-2) Grove of the Patriarchs, Ohanapecosh

Here and there we also see some maples which would add lovely colors to the grove in the fall.

This short and easy trail is great for anyone old or young alike to enjoy the tranquility of nature.

4) Paradise Area

The Adventure

Explore majestic views of Mount Rainier, subalpine meadows, cascading waterfalls, mighty glaciers and wildlife.

Getting There

Henry M. Jackson Visitor Center

39000 WA-706, Ashford, WA 98304

Tips

The **Skyline Trail** is the main trail in Paradise. Many trails start along this trail and although there are sign posts at junctions, be sure to carry a trail map (you can pick one up at the visitor center, ask for one at the park entrance or print it from home beforehand).

1) Skyline Trail to Glacier Vista (2.5 mile, 1,000ft elevation gain)

To hike up to Glacier Vista, start from the trailhead behind the visitor center and **head up the Skyline Trail clockwise**. You can take the **Deadhorse Creek Trail** and **Glacier Vista Trail** on the left side of the Skyline Trail at each junction then **head back to Paradise along the Skyline Trail** for magnificent views of Mt. Rainier, the Nisqually Glacier and the surrounding areas.

The first part of the trail is steep but gets better after the first half mile with many rewarding views.

2) Skyline Trail to Myrtle Falls (1 mile, 100ft elevation gain) and the **Nisqually Vista Trail (1.2 miles, 200ft elevation gain)** are easy trails that are accessible with strollers. For those who want to walk up for even more breathtaking views, the moderate hike along the Skyline Trail is worth the walk.

4) Paradise Area

Junior Ranger Program

Kids preschool age and up may enjoy participating in the **Junior Ranger program** to earn a **Junior Ranger badge**. Ask for a junior ranger activity book at the visitor center.

Paradise Area Trail Map

Source: http://www.nps.gov/mora/planyourvisit/upload/Paradise-Area-Trails-Aug11.pdf

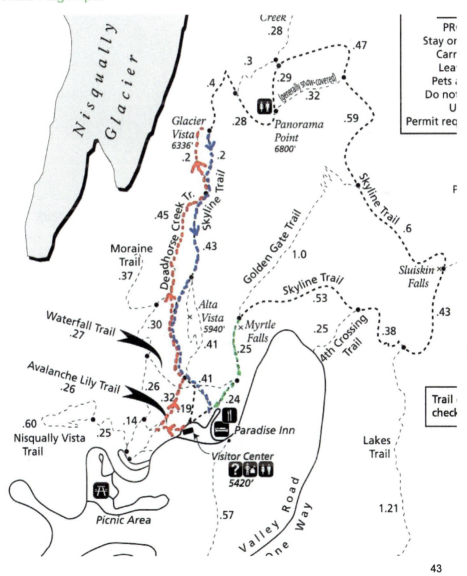

4-1) Skyline Trail to Glacier Vista, Paradise

We began our fourth day at Paradise to tackle the challenge of the Skyline Trail.

The words of conservationist John Muir are engraved on the stairs leading up to the main trailhead.

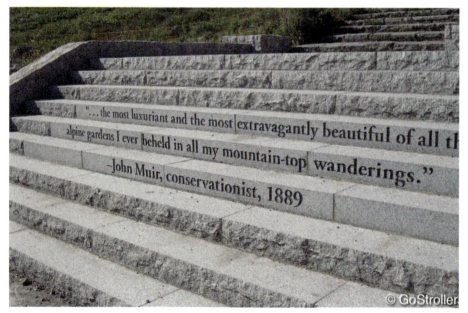

4-1) Skyline Trail to Glacier Vista, Paradise

Just like John Muir's words, summer at Paradise is at peak beauty with colorful wildflowers blooming in the green meadows, all with the Nisqually Glacier in the backdrop.

The Skyline Trail is one of the most popular trails at Mount Rainier. At a round trip of 5.5 miles (8.8km), it circles the whole Paradise area.

4-1) Skyline Trail to Glacier Vista, Paradise

However, the total elevation gain of this trail is 1,700ft (518m), which makes it a difficult hike even for adults. Therefore, we set our goal to complete about 1/3 of the trail, with Glacier Vista as our turnback point.

Beautiful weather and magnificent views are the perks of hiking in summer, but it also comes with challenges such as heat and bugs.

4-1) Skyline Trail to Glacier Vista, Paradise

All the while, when even a little critter such as a marmot crosses your path, you stop to watch and marvel at the wonders of the wildlife.

Continuing up the Deadhorse Creek Trail or Skyline Trail for about 1.5 miles (2.4km), you will find yourself getting closer to the Nisqually glacier.

4-1) Skyline Trail to Glacier Vista, Paradise

Looking back every once in a while, we see the winding zig-zag trail behind us and feel pride in how far along we have walked up.

Every step of the way, we learn to admire the beauty of nature and share our thoughts among each other.

4-1) Skyline Trail to Glacier Vista, Paradise

On clear days at Mount Rainier, you can see other mountains in the distance like Mt. Adams that looks a lot like Mount Rainier.

Mount St. Helens, the active volcano that most recently exploded in May, 1980, is another favorite landmark that we can see.

4-1) *Skyline Trail to Glacier Vista, Paradise*

When you reach Glacier Vista (elevation at 6,336ft (1,931m)), there is an area where you can stop to rest and enjoy the wondrous view of the glacier.

The view of the glacial waterfall and the roaring sounds of melting ice alone are well worth the slightly tough walk uphill.

4-1) Skyline Trail to Glacier Vista, Paradise

Among the people that we saw during the 4 hours we spent on this trail, our children were about the youngest ones there. Therefore, many people were encouraged when they saw such young kids.

It was a pleasant experience to see so many people hiking up the trail and how their faces glowed with joy as they headed back down after reaching their goal destination.

4-2) Skyline Trail to Myrtle Falls, Paradise

The waterfall trail, which is a short walk along the Skyline Trail towards the east to Myrtle Falls, is an easy trail good for families with young children.

The waterfall creates a beautiful view with the glacier topped mountain and the vibrant meadows.

4-2) Skyline Trail to Myrtle Falls, Paradise

If you cross the bridge across the waterfall and stroll along the Skyline trail for a bit, you can enjoy another great view of Paradise.

4-2) Skyline Trail to Myrtle Falls, Paradise

When you reach the fork for the Golden Gate trail (which cuts across the Skyline trail) you will meet a set of stairs heading up. The view of the mountain and meadow from this point is a beauty.

If you continue up the stairs, you will come across some snow on the meadows even during the summer.

4-2) Skyline Trail to Myrtle Falls, Paradise

The trees and wildflowers along with the snow capped mountain create a sublime view.

Just as the name implies, Paradise is indeed a heaven on earth which makes it the most popular destination in Mount Rainier National Park.

5) Longmire Area

The Adventure

Learn more about the history of Mount Rainier National Park at the Longmire museum, Longmire historic district and the Trail of the Shadows. Enjoy the short pleasant hike down to the Narada Falls Viewpoint.

Getting There

Longmire Museum, Mount Rainier National Park
39000 Washington 706, Ashford, WA 98304

Tips

1) Longmire Museum & Longmire Historic District
There is a suspension bridge that crosses the Nisqually River in the inner side of the Longmire Historic District. It is a short walk from the Longmire Museum through the Longmire Historic District which makes it a good turnback point when exploring the area.

2) Trail of the Shadows (0.7 mile round trip)
The Trail of the Shadows is an easy kid-friendly 0.7 mile (1.1km) loop trail that begins across the street from the Longmire Museum. The children loved seeing the trees that beavers chewed on. Start counterclockwise to see the historic sites first.

3) Narada Falls
Narada Falls is a short and easy 0.1 mile walk from the parking lot with a refreshing viewpoint of the falls. This is a nice stop on the way to or from Paradise.

Junior Ranger Program

Kids preschool age and up may enjoy participating in the **Junior Ranger program** to earn a **Junior Ranger badge**. Ask for a junior ranger activity book at the Longmire Museum.

5) *Longmire Area*

Longmire Area Trail Map

Source: https://www.nps.gov/mora/planyourvisit/upload/
Longmire_Cougar-Rock-Area-Trails-Aug11.pdf

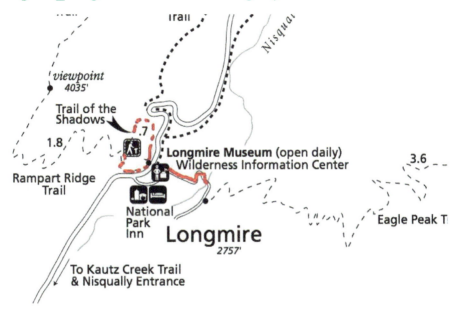

Narada Falls Area Trail Map

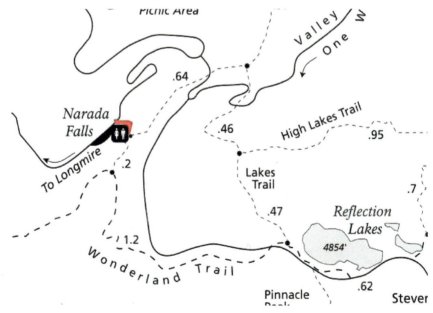

5-1) Longmire Museum, Longmire

At Longmire, you can learn about the history of Mount Rainier National Park at the Longmire Museum.

This area is a nice place to walk around and look at the exhibit in the museum if you have time.

5-1) Longmire Historic District, Longmire

At the Longmire Historic District, you can see the old vehicle that was used in 1937 to transport tourists.

The housing area in this district is currently used by the employees of the National Park Services.

5-1) Longmire Historic District, Longmire

If you walk past the housing area, you will reach the suspension bridge over Nisqually River.

A walk to this bridge which was constructed in 1924 to replace a smaller bridge is a nice easy stroll with the kids.

5-2) Trail of the Shadows, Longmire

The Trail of the Shadows is an easy 0.7 mile (1.1km) loop trail that is located across the street from the Longmire Museum.

You can see the remains of James Longmire's homestead and the hot springs along this trail which passes through the forest.

5-2) Trail of the Shadows, Longmire

When the volcano erupted 375,000 years ago, lava flowed down the Nisqually glacier, and later as the glacier melted over time, the meadow underneath it emerged.

The mineral springs smells like rotten eggs because of sulfur. You can also see the bubbles from the carbon dioxide gas, but in the past many people came to soak in the warm water and even drank the cold tonic.

5-2) *Trail of the Shadows, Longmire*

The Longmire Medical Springs Resort which opened in 1890 used to reside in the woods along the trail.

People came to enjoy the springs for its healing power and the views of Mount Rainier.

5-2) Trail of the Shadows, Longmire

This area where the meadow and forest meet is said to be an ideal environment for beavers. There are traces of beaver activity along the trail such as half cut trees.

This small cabin built in 1888 is the last remains of the James Longmire family's first settlement in Mount Rainier National Park.

5-2) *Trail of the Shadows, Longmire*

The children enjoyed crossing small wooden bridges and a partial boardwalk that also appear along the trail.

Along the marsh surrounding the water, you can also observe many interesting types of vegetation. From history to ecosystem, this light trail is full of learning opportunities.

5-3) Narada Falls, Longmire

The Narada Falls is a short 0.1 mile (0.2km) walk down from the parking area, making it a nice stopping point on the way to or from Paradise.

The waterfall drops 188ft (57m) in two tiers with the Mount Rainier Highway crossing it between the tiers. It also freezes in winter and is a popular attraction for ice climbing.

5-3) *Narada Falls, Longmire*

The sun shines down bright onto the powerful drop of the waterfall and the complete scene with the rainbow is absolutely beautiful.

6) Stevens Canyon Road Area

The Adventure

See reflections of Mount Rainier in the beautiful Reflection Lakes with an abundance of wildflowers in summer and experience a small part of the famous Wonderland trail down to Louise Lake. Enjoy the short (0.5 mile round trip) and easy trail to see the deep river-carved canyon.

Getting There

Reflection Lakes, WA 98361

Via Nisqually Entrance, Eatonville, WA 98328 or
Via Stevens Canyon Entrance, Randle, WA 98377

Tips

1) Reflection Lakes to Louise Lake (1 mile, 300ft elevation gain)

- If you follow the Wonderland Trail downhill for about **1 mile (about 300ft elevation)**, you can reach the **shore of Louise Lake** and enjoy the beautiful views along the trail and the shore.
- To head down to **Louise Lake**, walk east along **Stevens Canyon Road** until you get to the trailhead on your left, then head right at the first fork to continue unto the Wonderland Trail (refer to the Paradise Area Trail Map)

2) Box Canyon Loop Trail (0.5 mile round trip)

The second half of the **Box Canyon Loop Trail** is blocked by a fallen tree not far past the overlook bridge so you may have to turn back from there. (as of Aug 2016)

6) Stevens Canyon Road Area

Paradise Area Trail Map

Source: http://www.nps.gov/mora/planyourvisit/upload/Paradise-Area-Trails-Aug11.pdf

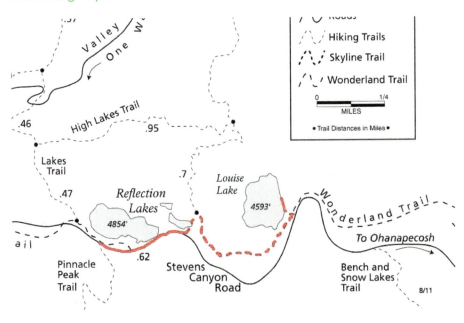

Box Canyon Loop Trail Map

6-1) Reflection Lake to Louise Lake

There is nothing quite like the feeling of excitement you get when you spend the night near the park and become one of the first people to enter early in the morning to enjoy the serene world of nature.

We began our last day at Mount Rainier National Park at the beautiful Reflection Lakes.

6-1) Reflection Lake to Louise Lake

Like the name implies, the Reflection Lakes are famous for the beautiful reflections of Mount Rainier in the waters. We walked past Reflection Lake to follow the trail down to Louise Lake.

To get there, you need to follow a part of the Wonderland Trail, which is the famous 93 mile (150km) trail that circles the whole park.

6-1) Reflection Lake to Louise Lake

You can get a glimpse of the lake from the trail that leads downhill for about a mile (1.6km). It was quiet and peaceful in the early morning hours.

Although we enjoyed the tranquility, we filled an empty water bottle with rocks to shake along the way in order to prevent any surprise encounters with wildlife.

6-1) Reflection Lake to Louise Lake

The trails within the park are maintained by not only the National Park Service but also by other non-profit organizations with many volunteers.

We felt gratitude to all those that help maintain these trails so that even the youngest explorers can easily enjoy them.

6-1) Reflection Lake to Louise Lake

Along the way, we passed a refreshing tiered stream and stopped to watch the cool water flowing down.

6-1) Reflection Lake to Louise Lake

After about a mile's walk (1.6km), we finally reached the lake that was viewable from above.

The final view of the lake through the trees before getting to the shore showed still waters and beautiful reflections of the surrounding trees.

6-1) Reflection Lake to Louise Lake

There was a sandy area at the shore of the lake where the children enjoyed playing with rocks, sticks and other toys that nature provided.

During the time we enjoyed here, we came across several hikers that stopped here for a short break while on their journey on the Wonderland Trail.

6-1) Reflection Lake to Louise Lake

We also discovered some footprints of wildlife on the sand and imagine how animals also come to the lake to enjoy what it has to offer.

The calm waters and the beautiful reflection of the surrounding trees provided a near private spot to relax in peace and quiet from the crowds that visit the park in the summer.

6-2) *Box Canyon Loop Trail*

While driving through Stevens Canyon Road, you can stop at Box
Canyon to walk a short loop trail and take a closer look at the canyon.

Box Canyon is a deep and narrow canyon carved by the Cowlitz River.
On the parking lot side, there is a wayside exhibit and on the other side
of the road, there is a short loop trail leading to an overlook bridge.

6-2) Box Canyon Loop Trail

Follow the 0.5 mile (0.8km) trail to get to a wide wooden bridge, which is the overlook to the canyon.

If you look down from this bridge, you can see the steep and narrow canyon as well as the fierce waters of the Cowlitz River below.

6-2) Box Canyon Loop Trail

The depth of this canyon to the water's surface is 115ft (35m). To see such a sight was like finding a hidden gem in Mount Rainier National Park.

Despite the rough waters below, the children joyously ran to and fro along the nice wide trail.

6-2) Box Canyon Loop Trail

The second half of the trail was blocked by a fallen tree so we turned back from there. (as of Aug 2016)

This light trail is a good place to stop while driving through the park for a short break to emerge in the powers of nature.

7) Carbon and Mowich Area

The Adventure

Explore the short (0.25 mile) Rain Forest Loop trail through a temperate rain forest and the largest and deepest lake in Mount Rainier National Park.

Getting There

Carbon River Ranger Station, Mount Rainier

35415 Fairfax Forest Reserve Road East, Carbonado, WA 98323

※ The Carbon River Road entrance is open to only hikers and bicycles (closed to vehicles) since the major flood of 2006.

Tips

1) Rainforest Loop Trail (0.25 mile round trip)

- Drive past the Carbon River Ranger Station to the end of the Carbon River Road and park at the trailhead to the Rain Forest Loop Trail.
- The Rain Forest Loop Trail is damaged a little past the half way mark so you may need to turn back from there.

2) Mowich Lake

To get to Mowich Lake you need to drive on an unpaved road for about 17 miles (27km), so be aware that it may become a hard journey without 4WD/AWD or if you do not have experience driving on unpaved roads.

7) Carbon and Mowich Area

Carbon River Area Trail Map

Source: https://www.nps.gov/mora/planyourvisit/upload/Carbon-River_Mowich-Area-Trails-Aug11.pdf

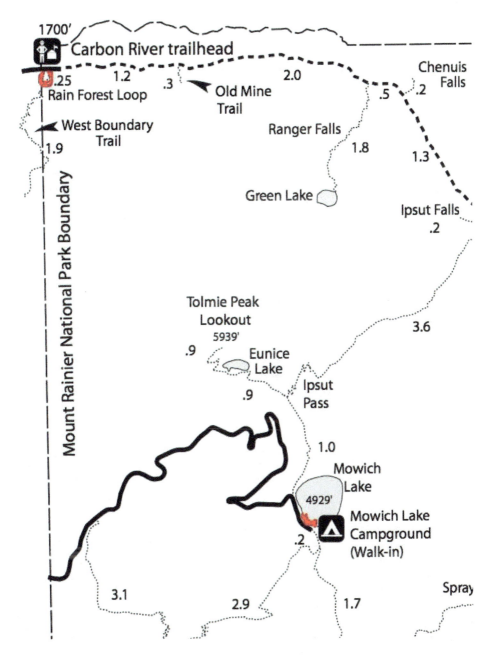

7-1) Rain Forest Loop Trail, Carbon River

Carbon River and the Mowich Lake area located on the northwest tip of Mount Rainier National Park is just 59 miles (94km) from Seattle, making it the closest location from the city.

The Carbon River Road was washed out by the flood in 2006 and is currently open to vehicles only up to the park boundary. Bicycles and pedestrians are allowed to explore the road beyond this point.

7-1) Rain Forest Loop Trail, Carbon River

If you park at the end of the road past the Carbon River Ranger Station, the trailhead is located on the right.

Slightly different from the rest of the park, the Carbon River area receives high amounts of rainfall year long. As a result, the climate and vegetation resemble that of a temperate rainforest.

7-1) Rain Forest Loop Trail, Carbon River

For those who have not visited the rain forest at Olympic National Park, this easy loop trail can give you a small taste of what a temperate rain forest looks like.

Part of this loop trail was damaged so we had to head back from that point but it was still nevertheless a nice stroll to experience the rain forest. (as of Aug. 2016)

7-2) Mowich Lake

Mowich Lake, the largest and deepest lake in Mount Rainier National Park, is about an hour's drive from the Carbon River area.

The uphill road leading to this area is unpaved after the first 3 miles for about 17 miles (27km). It is open only during the summer season and may be a rough drive without four wheel drive (4WD/AWD).

7-2) Mowich Lake

A far way up the rough road right before you reach the parking lot, you will come across a sign for Mount Rainier National Park, which cannot be found at any other area of the park.

Wildflowers bloom around the lake creating a beautiful scene while many campers from the campground enjoy swimming in the lake.

7-2) Mowich Lake

The clear blue waters of the largest as well as deepest lake of the park looks mystical as we walk along the shore to enjoy the views.

Although Mowich Lake is located in a less popular part of the park and not as easily accessible as other areas, it is a place with its own charm and beauty.

Epilogue

Before heading out on our journey, we thought that we had done enough research about Mount Rainier National Park and that we had prepared ourselves well for our adventure. Despite our plans however, we came across many sites that we had not even thought of and learned ever so much more about the area. We hope that the information gathered in this book will be helpful for other families that plan to visit the park. Thank you.

Go Strollers !!

Mount Rainier National Park

CPSIA information can be obtained
at www.ICGtesting.com
Printed in the USA
LVOW05s1729060617
537123LV00028B/279/P